A DAY THAT MADE HISTORY

THE DESTRUCTION OF POMPEII AND HERCULANEUM

C.A.R. Hills

Dryad Press Limited   London

Contents

THE EVENTS

THE INVESTIGATION

Acknowledgments

The author and publishers thank the following for their kind permission to reproduce copyright illustrations: Alinari, page 50; BBC Hulton Picture Library, page 47; Peter Clayton, pages 13, 16, 21, 32, 33, 45, 46, 53, 57, 58; Werner Forman Archive, pages 14, 15, 20, 24, 26, 27, 59, 60, 61; Mansell Collection Ltd, pages 1, 6, 8, 11, 22, 23, 48, 54, 55, 56; Photo Source Ltd, page 42. The maps and diagrams on pages 4-5, 10, 38, 39 and 52 were drawn by R.F. Brien. The illustrations were researched by David Pratt.

Cover photograph: Werner Forman Archive.

Title page picture: Vesuvius from the Forum of Pompeii (Mansell Collection).

The "Day that Made History" series was devised by Nathaniel Harris.

© C.A.R. Hills 1987. First published 1987.
Typeset by Tek-Art Ltd, Kent, and printed by R.J. Acford Ltd, Chichester, Sussex
for the publishers, Dryad Press Limited, 8 Cavendish Square, London W1M 0AJ

ISBN 0 8521 9696 2

THE EVENTS

Prelude to catastrophe: 24th August, AD 79, morning

The day on which the ancient Roman towns of Pompeii and Herculaneum were destroyed by an enormous eruption of the nearby volcano Vesuvius, 24th August, AD 79, began as not quite an ordinary day. Volcanic eruptions, particularly very large ones, tend to give advance warnings of themselves, and in modern times, when scientific understanding of volcanoes is well-advanced, these warnings are usually heeded and people moved away well in time. But until quite recently, such warnings were usually misunderstood or ignored, as seems to have been the case at Pompeii. It was perhaps not surprising: very few people even suspected that Vesuvius was a volcano at all.

Around the middle of that August, earth tremors had been felt, and on about 20th August these shocks had become severe, accompanied by a rumble as of distant thunder, which no-one yet suspected came from the mountain. Dogs barked without reason, birds were silent and fluttered here and there, wells ran dry, farmers anxiously searched the sky. But nobody knew what was to come.

Perhaps the inhabitants of the two towns and the countryside around them were more worried than they might otherwise have been, because seventeen years before, in February, AD 62, there had been an ominous warning of coming events: Pompeii and Herculaneum had been devastated by an earthquake. Earthquakes were frequent enough in the Bay of Naples region, but the destruction caused by this one had been particularly terrible: most public buildings in the two towns had collapsed, many people had been killed or had fled, and a flock of six hundred sheep had been entirely engulfed in a chasm that suddenly opened in the earth.

But the earthquake had lasted only a short time, and, after

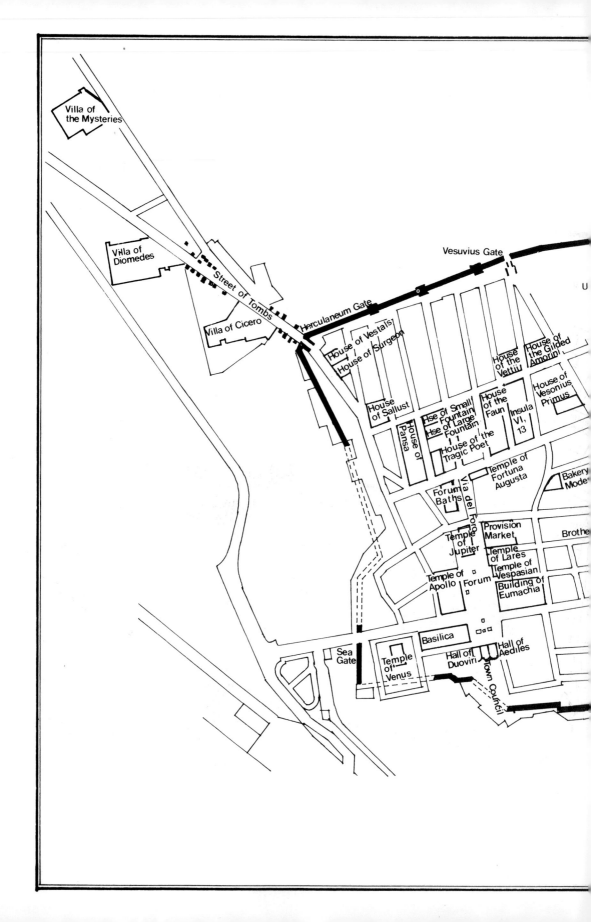

Villa of
the Mysteries

Villa of
Diomedes

Street of Tombs

Vesuvius Gate

Villa of Cicero

Herculaneum Gate

House of Vestals

House of Surgeon

House of the Vettii

House of the Gilded Amorini

House of Vesonius Primus

House of Sallust

House of Pansa

Hse of Small Fountain

Hse of Large Fountain

House of the Tragic Poet

House of the Faun

Insula VI, 13

Temple of Fortuna Augusta

Bakery Mode

Forum Baths

Via del Foro

Temple of Jupiter

Provision Market

Temple of Lares

Temple of Vespasian

Brothe

Temple of Apollo

Forum

Building of Eumachia

Basilica

Sea Gate

Temple of Venus

Hall of Duoviri

Hall of Aediles

Town Council

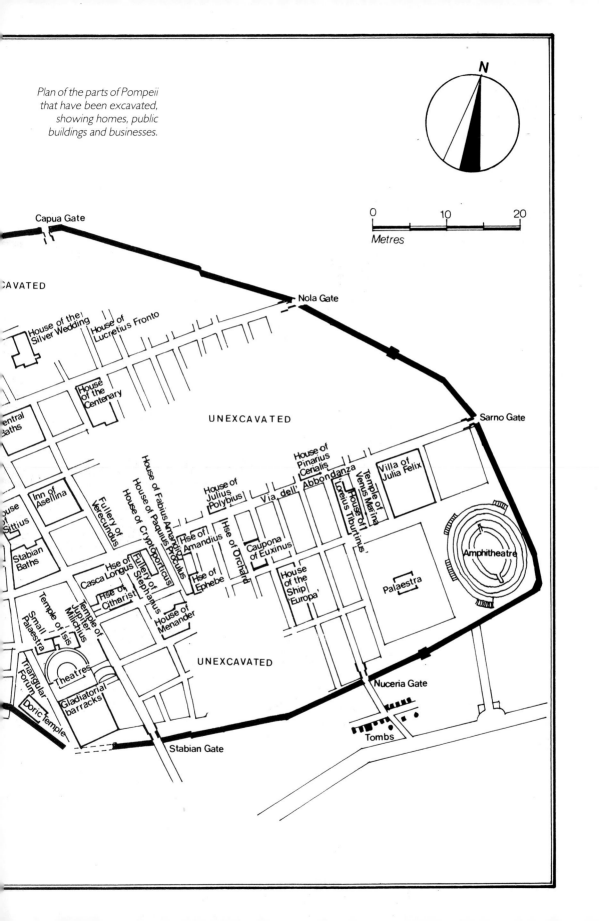

Plan of the parts of Pompeii that have been excavated, showing homes, public buildings and businesses.

N

0   10   20
Metres

Capua Gate

Nola Gate

CAVATED

House of the Silver Wedding

House of Lucretius Fronto

House of the Centenary

Sarno Gate

UNEXCAVATED

Central Baths

House of Pinarius Cerialis

House of Fabius Amandio

House of Paquius Proculus

House of Cryptoporticus

House of Julius Polybius

Via dell' Abbondanza

Temple of Venus Marina

Villa of Julia Felix

Inn of Asellina

Fullery of Verecundis

Hse of Amandius

Hse of Orchard

House of Loreius Tiburtinus

House of Sittius

Caupona of Euxinus

Fullery of Stephanus

Hse of Ephebe

House of the Ship 'Europa'

Amphitheatre

Casca Longus

Stabian Baths

Hse of Citharist

House of Menander

Palaestra

Temple of Jupiter Milichius

Temple of Isis

Small Palaestra

Nuceria Gate

Triangular Forum

Theatres

Gladiatorial barracks

Doric Temple

UNEXCAVATED

Tombs

Stabian Gate

some discussion, the inhabitants decided to return to their towns and face the slow, painful task of rebuilding them. After seventeen years this work was far from complete. In the Forum (main town square) of Pompeii many of the beautiful temples and grand public buildings still lay in partial ruin, while much of the town looked like a vast building site. But all

A panorama of Pompeii today, looking south-east from the Vesuvius gate.

this work was to be in vain. It is now thought that the earthquake of AD 62 represented an abortive attempt by Vesuvius to blast out an open vent for itself (the main crater was then completely closed). Seventeen years later it was to succeed, burying the half-reconstructed towns, as well as many villages and country villas, beneath an eruption of ash and rock, until they began to be dug up again more than 1600 years later.

Digging up the remains

Because, after the catastrophe, nothing was done to rebuild Pompeii and Herculaneum, and very little to dig up the remains of the towns from under the volcanic material, their sites became abandoned, and over centuries even their very existence was forgotten. The turbulent Italy of the medieval period (c.500-1500 AD) had little knowledge of and little interest in its ancient history. After 1500, with the intellectual movement called the Renaissance, interest in the ancient past grew, but still, for two hundred years, although there was some vague knowledge of the existence of the buried towns, almost nothing was done to excavate them. It was a chance incident – a peasant in the early eighteenth century digging a deep well and stumbling on remains of Herculaneum – which gave the impetus to the first digs. With a few intervals, digging has continued since then, slow and unsystematic at first, more scientific later. By the later twentieth century, about three-fifths of Pompeii has been uncovered, much less of Herculaneum.

Since their discovery, the towns have proved a uniquely detailed source of information about the everyday life of Italy at the time of the Roman empire. Also, because life in the whole of the empire – a vast area around the Mediterranean Sea and stretching from Scotland to Jordan – showed many common features, the towns are a vital source of information about the entire ancient world. Nowhere else have ancient towns been preserved, as here, virtually intact. For, after the initial violence of the eruption, which was anyway selective in its destruction, the volcanic material covering the towns acted more as a preserver than anything else: buildings remained where they stood, although perhaps without roofs; materials such as wood were simply carbonized, so that they remained, but in an altered state; cloth and papyrus (the ancient equivalent of paper) were scorched but not destroyed; and small objects such as egg-shells, loaves of bread, brooches, needles and shoes remained intact. Even the shape and general appearance of the people who died in the catastrophe have been preserved. Hollow spaces have been left in the ash, where people lay dead after they fell and, by pouring liquid plaster into the hole, letting it harden, and then removing the

Walnuts, a loaf and grain preserved by the volcanic ash that covered Pompeii.

surrounding ash, archaeologists gain a perfect replica of the body of a human being or animal at the moment of death. It is also possible to recover material objects in this way.

Thanks to these many types of remains, the life of Pompeii and Herculaneum is incomparably better-known to us than that of any place in the ancient world, and we also know more about the day of their destruction than about any other day in ancient times. From the remains of human bodies, it is possible to reconstruct exactly how and why they died, and both the remains and other pieces of archaeological evidence often tell us what they were doing immediately before catastrophe overtook them. In some cases, we even know the names and occupations, and have some personal information, about people who died and those who escaped. Modern scientific knowledge of vulcanism and the evidence of volcanic and archaeological remains enable us to build up a detailed picture of the course of the eruption, and we also have an important eyewitness record. So it is that the story of a day in two small, unremarkable towns almost 2000 years ago can be told in great detail.

Pompeii and Herculaneum in AD 79

The pattern of life in the two towns in AD 79 was peaceful, prosperous and, as far as we can tell, happy. The Bay of Naples region (otherwise called Campania) was one of the most favoured parts of the Roman empire. The line of coast starting one hundred and forty-five kilometres south-east of Rome, the empire's capital, and extending beyond the great city of Naples (Neapolis in ancient times) to the cape of Sorrento (Surrentum) was famous then, as it is now, for the extraordinary fertility of the land, and the beauty of its climate and scenery. Rich citizens of Rome, tired of the noise and dirt of the capital, had already begun to dot the landscape with their country villas, and the area had become a favourite spot for retirement. The great Roman writer Cicero, a hundred years before the catastrophe, had had a villa at Pompeii, of which he had been particularly fond; earlier in the first century AD, the beauty of the offshore island of Capri (Capreae, as it was then known) had tempted the emperor Tiberius (14-37 AD) to build a series of magnificent palaces there, where he could forget politics, leaving the care of Rome to his henchman, the cruel Sejanus.

Herculaneum lies to the west of Vesuvius, on the coast of

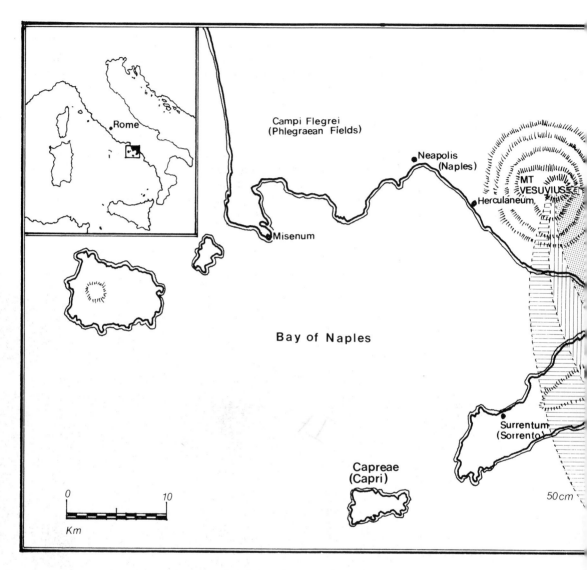

The map shows the area affected by the hail of pumice stones and the relative depths of ash ejected by Vesuvius in AD 79.

the bay, directly under the mountain and only about seven kilometres from its peak. Pompeii lies to the south of the mountain, a little further away from it, on the mouth of the river Sarno, and was nearer the coast in ancient times than it is now. The great city of Naples, which has tended to escape lightly in the successive eruptions of Vesuvius, lies to the north-west of both towns, about six kilometres from Herculaneum, about twenty-seven from Pompeii.

Pompeii and Herculaneum were already old in AD 79. It seems that they had both been founded in the eighth century

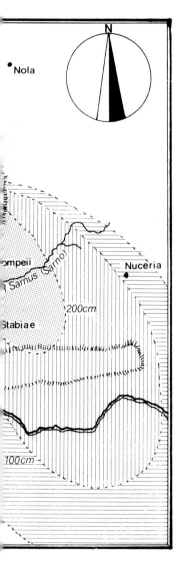

BC, by the Oscans, Italian tribes inhabiting the area and who spoke the Oscan language, related to Latin. Early in their history, both towns came under the influence, and perhaps the domination, of colonists from Greece, who founded many towns in Italy and brought a higher level of culture to what was then a backward peninsula. Greek influence was to remain strong, even when the towns fell successively under the domination of other Italian peoples aiming to control the peninsula: the Etruscans in the sixth century BC, the warlike Samnites, tribesmen from the hills of central Italy, and from 300 BC, the people of Rome, who had finally emerged victorious in the political struggles of Italy. In the last century before it was destroyed, Pompeii had little history: the only event of note, apart from the earthquake, was a brawl in the Pompeii amphitheatre in AD 59, with the people of nearby

In AD 59 a riot followed a gladiatorial contest in the amphitheatre at Pompeii and a number of spectators were killed or wounded. As a result, the senate in Rome banned all spectacles in the amphitheatre for ten years. This contemporary wall painting of the event was found in a house near the theatre.

Nuceria; this had led the Roman senate to forbid all shows in the amphitheatre for ten years.

By AD 79 Pompeii was one of the larger towns of provincial Italy, with about 20,000 people, a bustling port and trading town, with well-developed markets as far away as Gaul (modern France). It was well-known for the export of wine, made from grapes grown on the slopes of Vesuvius, and of *garum*, the fish sauce which was thought by the Romans to be indispensable for most dishes. Herculaneum was much smaller and quieter, with around 5000 people: it was a retirement centre and fashionable resort for the rich, while its poorer citizens were mainly fishermen.

Over these towns and the surrounding countryside Vesuvius towered, dignified and peaceful. We know now that it had last erupted in the Bronze Age, around 1200 BC, a time of which there were no records. Vesuvius (or Vesevus, as it was sometimes called in ancient times: both words were pronounced as if the V was a W) was a green mountain, covered with vineyards almost to its summit, where it was wooded. The geographer Strabo (64 BC-AD 19) had noticed that the mountain had a "cindery appearance" and rightly suspected that it was a volcano, but very few people shared his understanding. When the earth tremors began in August, AD 79, a few prudent inhabitants may have decided that it would be safer to leave, but there are no signs of a general exodus from Pompeii and Herculaneum.

20th-24th August, AD 79

After the disturbances of 20th August, the earth settled down in most places for a few days, and the fierce sun of a Mediterranean summer shone again over the blue waters of the beautiful bay. But on the night of 23rd August, it rained heavily and further tremors, worse than before, were experienced, which must have badly disturbed the Pompeians' sleep. Yet the morning of 24th August was cloudless once more and promised great heat; no doubt the people stilled their fears and prepared for the business of the day.

Roman daily life, for almost everyone, began at dawn. Not long after that time on this 24th August – "the ninth day before the Kalends of September", as the date was known to the Romans – Pompeii and Herculaneum would have sprung into vivid life. For some days one of the many Roman holidays had been in progress – the Festival of the Divine Augustus (the first of the Roman emperors, who had been made a god after his death) – and so the law-courts and public offices were closed, along with some businesses. There was no school either, as Roman children had almost four months' vacation every summer.

Nevertheless, Pompeii would have been crowded and colourful that day. At an early hour, the Forum would have been busy, with young men parading up and down, peasants from the outlying villages arriving to enjoy the sights, smart ladies passing in litters borne by slaves, and fortune tellers and street performers drawing the crowds. During these festival times, cycles of Greek and Roman plays were

Excavated Pompeii draws enormous numbers of tourists. These visitors are standing in the remains of the Forum – the religious, political and trading centre of the city.

This piece of tesselated (mosaic) pavement shows a masked actor preparing for a play. He may have been one of a band of strolling players who travelled from town to town providing a mixed show of music, dancing, juggling and mime.

presented at the theatres in the afternoon (mornings were set aside for rehearsals), while in the morning people could watch athletic events for boys which took place in the palaestras (exercise grounds). As midday approached, the winners in these events (naked in the fashion copied from the Greeks) would have been preparing to mount the podia to receive their olive-wreath crowns, watched by their elders from the shade of the loggias (spectators' stands).

The public baths opened towards midday. But the

amphitheatre of Pompeii was closed on this day: for when the combats to the death between professional fighters called gladiators, or wild-beast hunts, were on there, no other entertainment could compete. As lunch-time came, the many snack-bars of Pompeii began serving meals, rich women gave their orders to their slave cooks, while the women of the poor went to draw water for cooking from the public fountains.

It was around the sixth or seventh hour, Roman time (about twelve noon or one in the afternoon). Some people had already begun their lunch. In an elegant house overlooking the shore in Herculaneum, known to us as the House of the bas-relief of Telephus, servants were laying the table for a typical Roman lunch of hard-boiled eggs, bread, salad, cakes and fruit. In Pompeii, the priests of the Temple of Isis (an Egyptian goddess who had become popular throughout the Roman empire) were already reclining in the

The hot room (caldarium) of the Forum Baths at Pompeii. The floors and walls of the bath-house had ducts behind them which carried warm air – an early form of central heating.

Roman fashion in their *triclinium* (dining room), where the tables were laid with bread, wine, chicken, fish and eggs.

In the long street leading to the Nola Gate of Pompeii a group of gladiators were sitting in a tavern. They had with them a number of special trumpets, used for announcing events in the amphitheatre, and may have been larking around with them to amuse the other customers. Most of their fellow gladiators were back at their barracks, perhaps having spent the morning undergoing the strenuous training required of the men who risked their lives many times a year fighting in the amphitheatre. A richly-dressed woman was present at the barracks, maybe visiting a boyfriend. (The Roman gladiators enjoyed the sort of adulation given to pop stars today, and this must have compensated a little for their short life-expectancy.) Elsewhere in the barracks, two fighters had been locked up in the punishment cell – a reminder that discipline in these places was harsh.

In the graveyard outside the Herculaneum Gate of Pompeii, the descendants of someone buried there were celebrating a funeral feast-day, perhaps the anniversary of

Graves outside the Herculaneum Gate at Pompeii. A grave was considered to be the earthly home of the dead, revisited by them at certain times such as birthdays and other anniversaries. Groups of relatives would visit the tombs on these anniversaries.

their ancestor's death. They were having a meal, as was the Roman custom, in a beautiful chapel with wall-paintings adjoining the tomb. This tomb was also to become their own.

In one Pompeian bakery, the dough had just been mixed, and Modestus, the baker, had put eighty-one round loaves into his oven, as he had done many times before, to bake for an hour or so. But seventeen centuries were to pass before the loaves, reduced to charcoal, were to see the light of day. Modern researchers have ensured that the name of Modestus is not forgotten, nor that of Sextus Patulcus Felix, a Herculaneum baker who seems to have specialized in cakes and pastries, to judge from the charred contents of his oven. Nearby, at another bakery, where bread alone was made, two small donkeys wearing blinkers were walking round and round, turning a mill to grind flour. This was a job sometimes given to slaves, and particularly hated by them. But, this time, donkeys were tied to the mill to do the work, and no-one thought to release them in the panic: they were not animals on which people could ride away from the danger.

In the house of a Herculaneum gem-cutter, a sick adolescent boy lay on an elegantly veneered bed. A meal of chicken had been prepared for him, but it remained uneaten at his side. Now, after more than nineteen centuries, the bones of the unfortunate boy are still there on the bed for the tourists to gaze at fearfully. Not far from the Forum of Herculaneum, in the College of the Augustales (the priests in charge of the cult of Augustus), a man had flung himself on to the bed of another room from which there was to be no escape. He may have been a political prisoner, kept under lock and key, but this cannot be proved.

Also near the Forum of Herculaneum, a shipment of expensive glass had arrived and been placed under a colonnade. It was in a case packed with straw to protect it, but someone, perhaps the owner eager to see the new treasure, had ordered the case to be opened. A layer of straw was torn away to reveal a beautiful glass ladle.

In the house of a Pompeian fuller (cleaner of clothes), called Vesonius Primus, a dog, which we know to have been called Rufus, was tethered by a chain. No doubt he was used to being chained up, but he was soon to face forces beyond normal experience.

Suddenly the sound of an immense explosion rent the air. Once again, the earth shook, but more convulsively than before. Thousands of people stopped what they were doing, and must have shook with fear. The catastrophe had begun.

The fate of Pompeii: midday and afternoon, 24th August, AD 79

The first instinct, for those who were in their houses, must surely have been to run out into the streets, to see what could have happened. All eyes turned towards the mountain – Vesuvius was erupting. First great bursts of fire rose from it, followed by an immense black cloud, shooting up to an altitude beyond human sight, accompanied by deafening crashes. After hundreds of years of deceptive peace, Vesuvius was finally revealing its true character, of which it was to go on reminding mankind for another nineteen centuries. It was now an active volcano.

This explosion of AD 79, one of the largest in history, had thrust a great cloud of mingled ash, volcanic stones (lapilli), light volcanic rock (pumice) and poisonous gases more than twenty kilometres into the atmosphere. The prevailing wind on 24th August blew away from Herculaneum, but in the direction of Pompeii. It was on Pompeii therefore, that the great mass of this devastating material initially fell.

In the thunderstruck town, the sight of the immense cloud above Vesuvius was blotted out after only a short time, perhaps less than a minute. For suddenly it became as black as night – darkness at noon. A great barrage of objects began to fall from the sky: showers of stone, fragments of earth, great red-hot rocks, and with them a tearing rain. Flashes of lightning which intermittently cast an awesome light on the scene, and on the terrified faces of Pompeians shielding themselves from the pitiless bombardment from the air, also illuminated the forms of dead birds shot out of the skies.

Would the Pompeians have realized what was happening? Would they have known if the terror came from the sky or the earth? Lacking modern scientific knowledge, many inhabitants of the Roman empire led lives made miserable by superstition; by fear of the anger of the Gods, or of the end of the world. The eruption of Vesuvius may have seemed like the final catastrophe, blotting out Pompeii, Rome, Italy and all the provinces of the great empire.

As the immense pressure of steam and gases in the cavern of the volcano forced more and more material into the air, the hole at the top of Vesuvius soon became an enormous fire-crater. The winds blew the lighter pumice-stone and ash more than twenty-three kilometres from Vesuvius, blanketing the darkened countryside with the filthy debris. But the greatest violence, at this early stage of the eruption, was reserved for Pompeii.

The catastrophe was growing worse by the minute as the city was racked by a series of fearful shocks, and buildings began to collapse. The small stones that had rained down at first (about one centimetre in diameter) were succeeded after a while by larger rocks, up to twenty centimetres in diameter, which started fires where they fell. The first deaths in the town were probably caused by these larger rocks, falling from a great height upon people and buildings.

The lethal shower of rocks was not, however, the main cause of death in Pompeii: in fact, the majority of those who died were killed by asphyxiation. As people ran hither and thither in a panic, they were choked by an ash storm which burnt their hair and their mouths, making it almost impossible to breathe. Poisonous gases and fumes accompanied the thickly falling layer of ash, forcing many Pompeians to try to save themselves by hiding in locked or underground rooms. In most cases these proved to be death-traps: the victims were either buried alive, or choked by the ash and the gases which eventually penetrated their hiding-places.

It is interesting to ask yourself what you would have done if you had been faced with the dilemma of the Pompeians. Those who had swift horses probably decided that the best solution lay in immediate flight into the countryside. Others must have hoped to escape by sea; but the water was raging, and so much volcanic material was falling there that it would have been almost impossible to launch a boat. Some stopped to rescue their valuables, thus wasting precious time as the layers of lapilli and ash built up and it became more and more difficult to pass through the streets, or to escape from within buildings.

The gladiators in the tavern in the Via di Nola seem to have decided on immediate flight, leaving their trumpets behind in their escape. They were tough fighters, used to facing danger, and the Nola Gate of the town was close by – so perhaps they got away. But many of the other gladiators, who lived two to a room in sixty-six little cells around the courtyard of their barracks, were to die. The strict discipline there meant that a common policy was decided on. The decision was to stay put.

As the volcanic stones, and then the ash, began to fall ever more thickly on the town, the gladiators crowded together for protection in a few rooms. Thirty-four people were to meet their deaths in one room alone; in another, where the armour

19

Gladiators' barracks attached to the large theatre at Pompeii. The city had two semi-circular theatres (the other being the covered theatre) as well as an amphitheatre. Although the large theatre was probably designed for the performance of plays, gladiatorial contests and other popular entertainments were also staged there.

and helmets were stored, eighteen were to die – including the richly-dressed woman thought to have been visiting one of the men. Most of these people were asphyxiated by poisonous fumes and ashes. As for the two men chained in the punishment cell, they remained imprisoned and were miserably suffocated. A number of slaves working at the barracks had loaded a horse with clothes and valuables, but both they and the horse sank down dead before they could get away.

The priests at the Temple of Isis seem to have maintained in calamity the dignified calm befitting servants of the goddess. Their first action was to leave their meal and implore the help of Isis, by sacrificing at her altar. They next began to collect the precious objects of their temple – a large sum of money, including new coins of the emperor Titus (who had only come to the throne in the previous month), sacrificial vessels, and small statuettes. These they gave to one of their number, who hurried away carrying them in a linen sack.

The priest made for the Forum, but his bag was too heavy and he fell down under the rain of volcanic stones. Two more priests tried to escape across the Triangular Forum nearby, but just as they reached the shelter of some columns an earth tremor brought the masonry crashing down upon them. The rest of the priests stayed in the temple, where it seems that all of them were killed. They met various ends: one was caught between two falling walls, when he had already broken through two with an axe and was attempting to demolish a

The Temple of Isis, Pompeii. The cult of Isis, the Egyptian goddess of heaven and earth, life and death, was taken up by the Romans as a result of trading links and the military conquest of Egypt.

This silver plate was found among a complete set of 109 pieces at a country villa at Boscoreale, three kilometres north-west of Pompeii. The figure in the centre may be that of the original owner of the plate.

third; several others of the men collapsed beside the steps which led to the kitchen of the temple.

Publius Cornelius Tegetus was a man who had grown rich through trade and become a connoisseur of art, with many beautiful works in his house, including one statue, overlaid with gold, of an *ephebos* (a Greek youth undergoing his period of military training). His first thought was to save this

precious object, and so he had it brought in from the garden and covered with cloths. Perhaps he hoped to take it with him in his flight, but this proved impossible. He escaped with his household, leaving the statue behind.

In the house of Pansa, the inhabitants also gathered together precious things to take with them, including a bronze statue-group of Bacchus with a satyr. They had not gone beyond the garden before they realized that these pieces were too heavy to carry with them, and so they threw the bronzes into a copper cauldron that happened to be standing nearby. In another villa, at Boscoreale, just north-west of Pompeii, a slave carried a sack full of valuable silver plates to a room containing an oil-press, and there he dumped his burden in a well. In the House of the Philosopher, beautiful silver cups had been laid for a meal for guests, but apparently no-one thought it worth wasting the time to save them.

In the house of Vesonius, the unfortunate dog was still chained up: the family of the fuller had fled, without Rufus. As stones rained in through an opening in the roof of the room, the dog jumped as high as the chain attached to a

This watchdog, wearing a bronze-studded collar, was left chained up during the eruption that engulfed Pompeii. It suffocated beneath the ash and cinders which then hardened around the corpse. The body then disintegrated, leaving a perfect hollow mould. Giuseppe Fiorelli, the first person to systematically excavate the site (1860-75), developed a technique for making casts from these moulds by filling them with plaster.

bronze ring in his collar would let him, desperately trying to get free. In the end he was throttled. Quintus and Sextus, two sons of the banker Caecilius Iucundus, fled through this very house in order to reach the Street of Fortune: perhaps the dog was already dead by then. In the House of the Vestals, another dog died, having first become hungry and gnawed at his dead master's body. We know this because the man's bones bear the mark of the dog's teeth.

As the streets were piled higher and higher with ash and lapilli, it became increasingly difficult to escape. In the House of Menander, it is thought that some slaves hoped to get out through an upstairs window, or via the roof. Unfortunately, pumice and ash were already filling the building, and it seems

As the eruption continued some of the occupants of the House of Menander tried to escape by hacking a hole through a wall – but to no avail.

that ten of them died between the stairs and an upstairs door, including the leader who went ahead carrying a bronze lantern. One of the party hacked a hole in the wall of a room, but this did not help him escape. Meanwhile, the steward of the house, who would have had charge of the slaves, returned to his office by the entrance, carrying his master's seal and a purse full of money, and bringing with him his small daughter. Refusing to desert the house, he sat down on the bed, and held pillows over his own head and his daughter's, until both were suffocated by the fumes.

Seven children had gathered together in an upstairs room in the house of the baker, Paquius Proculus. Perhaps the children of the baker had been playing with their friends. All seven were killed when the upper storey collapsed over their heads, and buried them in its ruins in the room below. Next door, in the house of the priest Amandus, a whole family seems to have been killed, seeking refuge under the protection of the roof, unable to reach the street. Nearby, a number of people sheltering in a house with an underground hall decided to make a break for the open – but they too met their deaths, suffocated in the ash storm. One young girl desperately clung to her mother as both were asphyxiated.

In the Villa of Diomedes, just outside the town walls, there was a large underground cryptoporticus (underground storeroom with colonnades), where wine was stored in great jars. The master of the house decided that this cellar offered the best prospect of safety, and sent his wife, children and slaves down there with bread, fruit and other provisions. He himself took the house-key, a bag full of money, and one trusted slave, and hurried to the gate leading into open country, perhaps to try to find out if there was any hope of his family escaping by sea. At this gate, both master and slave fell down suffocated. Meanwhile, the thirty-four people in the underground rooms did not even touch their food: the ashes, bringing with them gases and poisonous fumes, soon asphyxiated them, as they had the head of the household.

The nearby Villa of the Mysteries, famous because it contains some of the most evocative paintings to have come down to us from the ancient world, was already half-empty. It had been badly damaged in the earthquake of AD 62, and the family of the house, the Istacidii, seem to have left their home in the care of a steward, Lucius Istacidius Zosimus. Perhaps it was he who wandered through the many rooms of the villa before taking refuge in a tiny watch-room, where he died, in a dark corner, gazing at the little finger of his left hand, on

Cast of the figure of a man
who died crouched in the
corner of a room.

which he wore an iron ring with a stone of chalcedony. Three women in an upper room died when the floors and roofs collapsed, plunging them through to the bottom storey. One of them, a young girl, still clutched a bronze mirror. Some workmen, busy with the reconstruction of the house, were suffocated in an underground hall. Altogether, eight people lost their lives in this great house.

Perhaps the grandest residence in Pompeii itself was that known to us as the House of Sallust; but wealth was no help to the last mistress of the house, who wasted time collecting bracelets, rings, a silver mirror and other treasured possessions, before dying outside her home as she attempted to flee. Beside her in the ash lay her three maids.

Even those who succeeded in making their way through the streets and reaching the gates of the town sometimes fared no better. Outside the Nucerian Gate, a beggar met his end; he was carrying a sack for alms and wore exceptionally good-quality sandals, which he may have received from public

A beggar, struck down at the Nucerian Gate, still wearing the good-quality sandals he had probably been given by a public charity.

charity. Near the Nola Gate a man climbed a tree and died in its branches. The great mass of fugitives must have fled towards the Herculaneum Gate, because this was the quickest way to try to escape by sea, but here there was mad chaos, and many corpses have been found piled up on each other near this gate.

The corpses of around 2,000 people have been discovered in Pompeii: roughly a tenth of its population. How many more were killed in the open countryside, borne down by poisonous fumes? How many more died in boats on the furious sea? We can never know. But we can be certain that a good number succeeded in escaping to nearby towns, because we know of relief measures and new homes being organized for them.

By late afternoon, it is difficult to believe that anyone still breathed in Pompeii itself. Still the downpour of stones and ash continued, with fewer stones, but great layers of ash, which were to bury the town to a depth of 17 metres. Lethal electric flashes continued to illuminate the ghastly scene, but the town of Pompeii, once so happy and prosperous, had begun its 1600 years of sleep.

The response of Pliny the Elder: afternoon, 24th August, AD 79

Most of those who met death at Pompeii were ordinary people, of whom we would never have heard if death had not given them a name. But it so happens that, near the scene of the catastrophe, there were also present two of the more famous personalities of Roman history – the uncle and nephew, both writers and public servants, known to us as Pliny the Elder and Pliny the Younger. In two celebrated letters, written many years afterwards to the famous historian Cornelius Tacitus, who was writing a history of the period, Pliny the Younger described his uncle's tragic death and his own experiences at the time of Vesuvius's eruption.

The Plinys were wealthy landowners from the neighbourhood of Lake Como, in northern Italy. They were not of the ancient nobility, but Gaius Plinius Secundus (Pliny the Elder) had risen as high as was possible in the second (equestrian) rank of the imperial service. When Vesuvius exploded, he had recently been appointed commander of the Roman Navy by the new emperor Titus, and was stationed at Misenum (modern Punto di Miseno), which lies at the extreme north-western end of the Bay of Naples, at some distance from Vesuvius. The elder Pliny was also well-known as a writer and expert on natural science. The younger Pliny, also named Gaius Plinius Secundus, was seventeen at the time, a studious youth (he had written a "tragedy" in Greek at the age of fourteen), who was to rise to become a senator, governor of the province of Bithynia and one of the most famous letter-writers of ancient Rome. When Vesuvius erupted, he and his mother were staying with his uncle at Misenum.

It seems that Misenum was too far away from Vesuvius for the initial eruption to be heard there, but the younger Pliny tells us in his letter to Tacitus that, in the early afternoon of 24th August, his mother drew his attention to "a cloud of unusual shape and appearance". The elder Pliny, who had taken a cold bath, had lunch and was working at his books, called for his shoes and climbed to a high place to observe the cloud. The younger Pliny describes it:

> "Its general appearance can best be expressed as being like an umbrella pine, for it rose to a great height on a sort of trunk and then split off into branches . . . . In places it

looked white, elsewhere blotched and dirty, according to the amount of soil and ashes it carried with it."

The elder Pliny's scholarly curiosity about natural phenomena was aroused; he ordered a boat to be made ready so that he could inspect the cloud at closer quarters. He told his nephew that he could accompany him, but the bookish younger Pliny said that he would prefer to continue with his studies – his uncle had given him some writing to do.

As the elder Pliny was leaving the house he was handed a message from a woman called Rectina, who lived in a house near the sea, at the foot of Vesuvius, from where escape would only be possible by boat. She was terrified, and begged the elder Pliny to come and rescue her. How she had succeeded in getting the message to him, we are not told, but perhaps a neighbour had left the area by boat at the time of the eruption. The elder Pliny's aim in sailing towards Vesuvius now became more than merely scientific: he wanted to rescue Rectina, and as many other people as possible, and ordered warships to be made ready for this purpose. Fearlessly, he went on board himself and made straight for the danger zone.

With proverbial Roman courage and detachment, Pliny the Elder occupied himself in making notes of the phenomena he observed as his ship sailed on into an area where hot ashes and blackened volcanic stones were already falling. He probably sailed past Pompeii in mid-afternoon, by which time the tragedy of the town would already have been complete, leaving no-one there alive.

It proved impossible to reach Rectina, because suddenly the ships entered shallow waters where the shore was blocked by the debris from Vesuvius. The helmsman of Pliny's ship advised turning back. Pliny considered this, but replied with the Roman proverb "*Fortes fortuna invat*" – "Fortune favours the brave" – and decided to make for the house of his friend Pomponianus at Stabiae (modern Castellamare di Stabia, six kilometres south of Pompeii), a place which the shower of ashes had not yet fully engulfed.

The frightened Pomponianus had already put his belongings aboard ship, and was hoping to escape over the hazardous sea. But Pliny the Elder encouraged his friend, making light of the danger they were in. Pliny had his bath, ate dinner with Pomponianus and then went to sleep at the normal hour of around six or seven in the evening. His nephew, who heard about these events later, comments, "He was quite cheerful, or at least he pretended he was, which was no less courageous."

The end of Herculaneum: evening and night, 24th August, AD 79

Our knowledge of the end of Herculaneum has changed substantially in the last few years. Until recently only about thirty skeletons had been found in Herculaneum, and it was thought that a river of volcanic mud which had begun to surge towards the town soon after the eruption had forced almost the entire population to flee in the direction of Naples. But in the light of fresh discoveries at the marina of Herculaneum, and recent research into the nature of the material which overwhelmed the town, a new and more terrible picture has developed of the end of this elegant settlement.

It now seems that, in the afternoon of 24th August, the prevailing wind blew towards Pompeii and not Herculaneum, and so the initial damage to the smaller town was slight. Nevertheless, the eruption so nearby, and the earth tremors, must have been horrifying. There was also, during the afternoon and evening, a fall of pumice and ash, but it was light, and did not threaten life. Probably only twenty centimetres fell during the twelve-hour period in which Pompeii was all but overwhelmed by the material.

The citizens of Herculaneum were in a strange dilemma. Death did not seem to threaten them immediately, and, as long as the direction of the wind did not change, the main road to Naples – six kilometres away – would not have been impassable. As it happened, Naples was to escape during the whole eruption with only a light blanket of ashes and some earth tremors. A large number of people must have thought that flight to Naples was the best course, but it was as black as night, with the darkness broken only by electric flashes accompanying the sudden earth shocks. Many, it seems, thought it best to stay at home, and for these citizens there was to be no escape.

It is thought that around midnight Vesuvius released over its rim new and infinitely more destructive materials, travelling at tremendous speeds. Although these included some volcanic mud, they were mainly ground surges and pyroclastic flows, the second phase of the eruption, following the deposits of pumice, lapilli and ash. A ground surge is a turbulent cloud of volcanic ash and hot gases, which may travel at more than ninety-five kilometres an hour, hugging the ground as it goes. Pyroclastic flows, also moving at great speed, are hot, dry, chaotic avalanches of ash, pumice and volcanic gases. The two occur in close combination with each other – the ground surge may go slightly before – and mean inevitable death and destruction to anyone or anything in their path. Herculaneum lay just beneath Vesuvius, on a promontory between two streams of volcanic material. Pouring down the slopes of the mountain the full force of these flows hit the town. It seems highly unlikely that anybody in Herculaneum at that hour can have escaped death.

The end must have come within minutes. The ground surge and pyroclastic flow swept into the town with irresistible force, hurling roof tiles, statues and small objects down the streets, tearing columns from their bases, and bursting through walls. Yet, despite the force of the flows, their action, in regard to material objects, was strangely selective: some streets remained protected by their position, and many small and perishable objects remained essentially unharmed. The effect for human beings, however, was unequivocal: the inundation of the town continued until Herculaneum was submerged to a depth of more than 19 metres.

We know something about many individual tragedies. The sick boy still lay in his bed in the house of the gem-cutter. Had he been deserted by his family? It is easy to imagine his fear

Shops in the main street of Herculaneum.

Entrance to the House of the Stags, Herculaneum.

as he faced the fall of night all alone, and terrible to think what his last moments might have been like. The man whom we believe to have been locked up in the College of the Augustales also died, trapped in his tiny room. Two bodies were discovered seven and a half metres above the level of one ancient street: they must have been tossed far upwards by the oncoming surge.

A great frightened crowd had gathered at the marina of Herculaneum, perhaps fearing the impending catastrophe and hoping for a swift escape by sea. They were probably awaiting the arrival of fishing boats, or ships of the Roman Navy. A large number of people sought safety in the vaulted underground chambers opening out onto the shore, which were used for storing boats in winter. It seems that some boats were launched, despite the extreme violence of the sea, for we know that one vessel, 10 metres long, capsized, no doubt killing all who were in it. The body of one drowned man has been found, still clutching an oar.

When the ground surge came, the frightened crowd at the marina must have been overwhelmed almost immediately, in a violent death of asphyxiation in which human bodies were tossed over long distances, their limbs flailing. Huddled together in death, a family of seven adults and four children perished, along with a baby of seven months, held by a girl of around fourteen. Torn from them in their final moments were a lamp, the key to a house, and a coin box with a combination lock containing only two coins – perhaps a child's small savings. Another child led her pet horse down to the beach, where both were to die.

One woman was blown off a terrace 20 metres above the marina: her shattered body was found on the beach. A Roman soldier, hefty and well-fed like most men in the legions, was slammed to the ground face-down over his sword and scabbard. Under an archway, a woman wearing jewelled rings on her left hand and golden bracelets and ear-rings fell dead in all her finery. Another young woman of around twenty-five was seven months pregnant when she died. A patch of hair on her skull has revealed that she was blonde. More than one hundred and fifty skeletons have been found on this beach of death, belonging to people of different classes, ages and life-experiences, who found equality in the terrible moments when disaster overtook them.

The experiences of the two Plinys: night, 24th August, and morning, 25th August, AD 79

We left the younger Pliny in the early afternoon, watching his uncle set sail before continuing his studies. He spent the rest of the day with his books, the catastrophe still seeming distant. In the early evening he took a bath, had dinner, and dozed fitfully for a while.

But suddenly the earth at Misenum was rent by new and even more violent tremors. Pliny's mother rushed into his room and found him just in the process of getting up. They sat down in the forecourt of the house, by the sea, not knowing what to do. Finally, the young man ("I don't know whether I should call this courage or foolishness on my part") sent a slave to fetch a volume of the historian Livy and went on with his studies. One of his uncle's friends scolded them both for just sitting there, but Pliny the Younger remained absorbed in his book.

At last, when the buildings around them were already tottering and the house seemed in imminent danger of collapse, they decided to leave the town, and were followed by a panic-stricken mob of people looking for someone to give a lead. Beyond the buildings of the town they saw the sea being sucked away and forced back by successive earth tremors, and also, much nearer to Vesuvius, "a fearful black cloud rent by forked and quivering bursts of flame". This, it seems, was the ground surge which had recently destroyed Herculaneum, but was fortunately not to reach Misenum.

The young man's mother urged him to make his escape as best he could, because ash was now starting to fall thickly and the dense black cloud seemed to be moving towards them. She said that she herself, old and slow, could only die in peace if she knew that he had escaped. Pliny refused to leave her, and instead took her by the hand. Pitch darkness fell as they went on, and they sat down to rest for the night. In Pliny's own words,

"You could hear the shrieks of women, the wailing of infants and the shouting of men; some were calling their parents, others their children or their wives, trying to recognize them by their voices. People bewailed their own fate or that of their relatives, and there were some who prayed for death in their terror of dying. Many asked the help of the gods, but still more imagined there were no gods left, and that the universe was plunged into eternal darkness for evermore."

Now, more than 1900 years later, we can only imagine the terror and superstitious fear of those people wandering the roads around the Bay of Naples.

At last the darkness thinned: it was morning, and a pale, yellowish sun shone, as during an eclipse, illuminating a countryside buried deep in ashes like snowdrifts. Pliny and his mother returned to Misenum, where they anxiously awaited news of his uncle, who had been so much closer than they to the scene of the catastrophe.

At Stabiae, near Pompeii, the elder Pliny had also slept. But the catastrophe was coming closer, and the courtyard giving access to his room was piling higher and higher with ash. At some point before dawn he was roused, and joined Pomponianus and the rest of the household, who had stayed up all night. They debated whether to stay indoors or to take their chance in the open, until the violent earth shocks finally drove them outdoors, pillows tied to their heads as protection against the volcanic stones.

It was now dawn, and while at Misenum it was daylight, at Stabiae it was still as black as night. The elder Pliny decided to go down to the shore to see if a boat could be launched, but the sea was still too dangerous. Here the old man, who was heavy for his age, began to choke, calling repeatedly for cold water to drink. Flames and a smell of sulphur were penetrating the beach, and the party of people there decided to flee. Pliny the Elder stood up, leaning on two slaves, but suddenly collapsed to the ground, asphyxiated by the poisonous fumes. There his body lay, as his nephew heard later, "looking more like sleep than death".

It was 25th August. During that day the eruption continued, and ashes spread even further from the area of the volcano. The smoke, composed largely of stones and ashes, was to drift for days like clouds, and fine ash was eventually to reach as far as the coast of North Africa and the Middle East. For the whole of this second day most of the area around Vesuvius was still in darkness, but on the third day the sun shone again, and the terrible black cloud separated into long strips, which then scattered.

The landscape revealed by the returning sun was utterly transformed: great areas south and east of Vesuvius were covered with white ash, like a massive layer of snow. Pompeii and Herculaneum, as well as many villas and smaller villages such as Oplontis and Taurania, had almost entirely vanished from the earth, only the highest rooftops rising out of the ground here and there to remind people that a happy and prosperous life had once existed. It is thought that Vesuvius too had changed its shape: it now had two peaks, one entirely new, from which white smoke was rising. Forty-eight hours before, not a puff of smoke had ever been seen within human memory to come from the mountain's crater, but Vesuvius was not to shroud its nature in secrecy again.

THE
INVESTIGATION

Why did Vesuvius explode?

In order to understand the eruption of Vesuvius in AD 79, it is necessary to know something about the way that volcanoes work in general, and about the different types of volcanic eruptions, with their very different consequences for the particular environments and human beings involved.

Volcanoes and mountains

A volcano may be defined essentially as a rift or vent through which *magma* (molten rock material highly charged with gases) is discharged from within the earth. Magma erupts

This diagram shows the mechanism of a Vesuvian-type eruption, where material which has long been held under pressure in a central vent erupts to form a huge mushroom-shaped cloud.

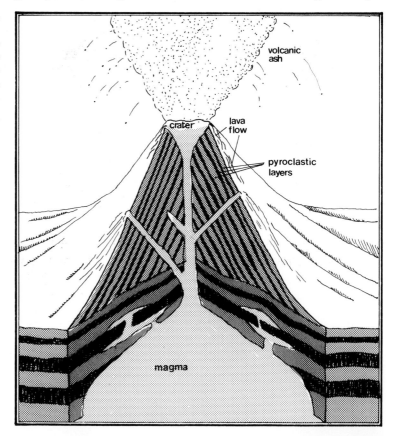

volcanic ash

crater   lava flow

pyroclastic layers

magma

either as flows of red-hot *lava* (molten rock) or as explosive clouds of volcanic ash, stones and gases. A volcano is most usually a mountain, and many high mountain ranges throughout the world consist mainly of chains of volcanoes built by lava or ash. In other cases, vulcanism (the general term for volcanic activity) and other earth-building processes may have combined to form a mountain range.

A striking fact about volcanoes is that they are far from evenly spread around the earth. Almost all the volcanoes in the world occur within a couple of hundred kilometres from the sea, and in fact they are concentrated in certain well-defined areas. Typically they occur in long, narrow chains. This reflects the fact that volcanoes, like earthquakes and other symptoms of earth disturbance, are associated with parts of the earth currently experiencing mountain-building activity.

This map shows the world's tectonic plates and the zones of collision between them, which are typically areas of mountain-building, earth disturbances and vulcanism.

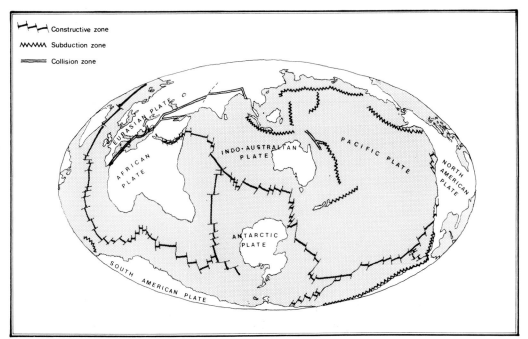

Constructive zone

Subduction zone

Collision zone

Plate tectonics Our understanding of mountain-building has been revolutionized since the late 1960s by the theory of *plate tectonics*. This visualizes the earth's crust and the upper part of its mantle as a set of rigid plates, resting on a weaker and deformable layer below. The plates underlie the oceans and continents, and move in relation to one another. Most features of mountain-building, such as volcanoes and earthquakes, occur where the plates border one another. The Mediterranean, near which Vesuvius is situated, is one such area, lying on the boundary between the Eurasian plate and the African plate.

Continental material is continually being created or destroyed, at the boundaries between the plates. A *constructive* plate margin is where new material is pushed upwards, while a zone of *subduction* is where the material is taken back within the earth's mantle. In the Mediterranean area, two plates are in collision, owing to the subduction of material, although it is thought that subduction has now largely ceased. This explains why volcanic and earthquake activity is now mild; those earthquakes that occur are shallow-focus (the point of release of the earthquake is not deep within the earth's crust), and volcanic activity is confined to the region of the Appenine mountains (within which Vesuvius lies) and around the Aegean Sea. Apart from Etna, Vesuvius is now the only active volcano in Europe, although it lies within a great chain of dormant and extinct volcanoes running down the coast of Italy. This chain includes the Phlegraean Fields near Naples, which consist of low craters with hot, bubbling springs and scalding blasts of steam.

Types of volcanic eruption Volcanic material produced in zones of subduction is described as *andesitic* in chemical composition, while that produced by upward movement is termed *basaltic*. Eruptions of the basaltic variety typically give rise to free-flowing streams of lava, whereas andesitic eruptions tend to consist of thicker lava sheets, volcanic ash and pyroclastic material (fragmented volcanic rock). This is because, in the process of subduction, a great deal of other matter is added from within the earth's crust. At Vesuvius, in AD 79, there was, in fact, no flow of red-hot lava, the material most commonly associated with volcanic eruptions. Pompeii was overwhelmed by volcanic ash, Herculaneum by a ground surge and pyroclastic flow.

The shape of volcanoes and of their eruption varies greatly. In some cases volcanoes may not be mountains at all, but lava may erupt in a relatively mild but continuous manner through a series of fissures in the earth. Such eruptions rarely involve much danger to human lives or property. An eruption of the Vesuvian type is different. Here, the characteristic feature is an extremely violent expulsion, from a central vent, of magma which has become highly charged with gas during a long period of superficial quiescence or mild activity. When the overhead pressure on the underlying magma is finally relieved, the magma bursts upwards into a cauliflower-shaped cloud, distributing showers of ash and stones over a wide area. This is what happened at Pompeii in AD 79.

Vesuvian eruptions   An eruption of the Vesuvian type may have various phases. The first phase – which destroyed Pompeii – is known as the *Plinian* phase. This includes the stupendous blast of uprushing gas many kilometres into the air, and the spreading cloud dropping volcanic ash and stones. It may be followed – as it was in AD 79 – by a *Peléan* phase, in which a very high degree of explosiveness is reached, and material is ejected in pyroclastic flows, often taking the form of an enormously fast-moving cloud called a *nuée ardente* (burning storm-cloud). Such explosions are of particularly great danger to human life, as shown at Herculaneum in AD 79, and also in the most famous eruption of this type – the destruction in 1902 of the city of St Pierre by Mount Pelée on the island of Martinique. There, as at Pompeii and Herculaneum, preliminary warnings were ignored or misunderstood, and a pyroclastic flow overwhelmed the town, killing all but two of its 28,000 inhabitants. These two were in tightly sealed rooms at the time of the disaster. One of them – probably the most famous survivor of a volcanic eruption – was a prisoner in the town jail. In this case, the pyroclastic flows were not accompanied by a previous eruption of Plinian type, as in AD 79.

Vesuvius since AD 79   The eruption of AD 79 put an end to Vesuvius' period of quiescence, and marked the start of a new active phase. The eruption was ten times the size of one of the most devastating of recent times, that of Mount St Helens in 1980. It is thought, although it has been disputed, that the eruption of AD 79 changed the shape of the volcano, giving it two peaks instead of one, the extinct Mount Somna being joined by the new active crater.

In the first sixteen centuries following the eruption of AD 79, Vesuvius broke into violent eruption only ten times, each explosion being followed by another period of quiescence. Then, in 1631, after 130 years of rest, an extremely violent eruption occurred. Second only to that of AD 79 in loss of life and damage caused, this started a fresh cycle of volcanic activity, with eruptions every thirty years or so. Major explosions occurred in 1872, 1906 and 1944, and a small earthquake was sparked off by Vesuvius in 1980.

It may seem strange that, despite the violence of Vesuvius,

The eruption of Vesuvius in March, 1944. The city of Naples is in the foreground. The lava flow caused by the eruption engulfed the villages of Massa and San Sebastiano.

the Bay of Naples area is and always has been heavily populated. This reflects the dual nature of volcanoes as sources sometimes of danger and death but also of benefit to humankind. Volcanic soil (as found in the Bay of Naples region) is usually extremely fertile; volcanoes provide energy and material for industry; moreover, they often form areas of great natural beauty (and of few places is this more true than of the area around Vesuvius). Most volcanoes are not in fact dangerous, and so people are not foolish to settle near them. The complex nature of the volcano, source of both good and bad, is perhaps especially evident in the eruption of AD 79. We should never forget the terrible suffering of those who died and those who mourned them, but from this evil some good has come. The catastrophe preserved these beautiful towns and has thus given us a unique and infinitely pleasurable contact with our ancient ancestors.

How did we find out about Pompeii and Herculaneum?

The story of the discovery of Pompeii and Herculaneum is closely linked to the development of the modern science of archaeology – the study of the remains of our past, often accomplished through the *excavation* (or digging-up) of towns or villages that have become buried in the course of time. The rediscovery of the buried cities of Campania in the eighteenth century was the first major modern excavation, and the site continues to be among the most important archaeological works in progress today. We can see the whole history of modern archaeology mirrored in the work at Pompeii, from the earliest, highly unscientific attempts, when a quest for loot was the main motive for digging, to the highly sophisticated (although still problem-filled) methods of today.

The Pompeians return
The very earliest excavations were made not in the eighteenth century, but by the Pompeians themselves. At an early stage, the decision was taken that, since there had been two major disasters – the earthquake and the eruption – it was best not to try to resettle the area of the towns. A substantial disaster relief programme, personally authorised by the Emperor Titus, was directed mainly at settling homeless people in nearby cities such as Naples. But it is clear that some Pompeians went back to their town as soon as it was safe, to dig down for precious belongings or to try to recover the bodies of loved ones. These people left graffiti to record their presence: one macabre epitaph, presumably referring to bodies of the dead, reads: "There were fifty of them, still lying where they had been." These people who returned to Pompeii succeeded in removing many statues, marble facings and personal belongings from the wreckage, and this is one reason why not as many objects were later recovered at Pompeii as we would have liked. At Herculaneum such digging was impossible because of the depth and solidity of the volcanic material, and all that had not been destroyed in the eruption remained on the site.

The end of the Roman empire
The eventual rediscovery of the towns was to be a long time coming. The disaster initially provoked great interest within the Roman empire; after all, an area had been destroyed where many eminent Romans had country homes. The poets

Martial and Statius wrote mournful verses commemorating the event, and a century afterwards the historian Dio Cassius wrote a detailed account of the eruption of Vesuvius.

As time passed, the Roman empire became overwhelmed by fighting barbarian tribes, and finally disappeared. For many hundreds of years, life in Europe was less civilized and developed than it had been under Rome, and gradually the very existence of the buried towns was forgotten by everyone. For a thousand years, the only reminder of them was the name given to the low hill under which Pompeii lay: it was called, in Italian, *cività* (the city). But this did not mean that people had any real idea that a city was in fact buried there. On the site of Herculaneum, a town developed, called Resina. In modern times it has been renamed Ercolano, the Italian equivalent of its Latin name.

The first sighting From the fifteenth century onwards, in the period called the Renaissance (*rebirth*), a great interest developed in ancient Greece and Rome, as it was thought that these civilizations might have much to teach the modern world. Nevertheless, the first discovery of Pompeii was accidental, and not followed up. In 1594, an Italian architect called Domenico Fontana was at work constructing a channel to divert the river Sarno, to bring water to the villa of a nobleman. While this was going on he stumbled upon some walls of ancient Pompeii bearing Latin inscriptions. The very word "Pompeii" was seen, but misunderstood: it was thought that a villa belonging to the Roman statesman Pompeius had been found. Surprisingly enough, no attempt was made to follow up this remarkable discovery.

The Prince d'Elboeuf The eventual start of continuous excavation at the towns also came about by a sort of accident. One day in 1709, a Resina peasant was digging a deep well when he hit upon costly stone of all kinds – the remains of ancient Herculaneum. He gave little thought to the matter, but his discovery was brought to the attention of the Austrian Prince d'Elboeuf (the Austrians were then in control of that part of Italy), who bought up some land over Herculaneum and began digging. His tunnelling parties eventually discovered part of the town's ancient theatre, then in an almost perfect state of preservation, fittings and all. Unfortunately, the prince was interested only in plundering the site: he removed anything precious that he found, and kept no records. Later in the eighteenth century, the danger from poisonous gases meant that the tunnels leading to the theatre had to be abandoned, and it has never been possible to excavate the theatre since then.

Scientific excavation The prince's discovery marked the beginning of a more general interest in Pompeii and Herculaneum. The King of Naples, Charles III, who came to the throne in 1734, heard about the towns, and appointed a Spanish engineer and officer, Roque de Alcubierre, to begin excavations at Pompeii. The labour force, partly composed of convicts,

Charles III, Bourbon King of Naples, who initiated the first systematic excavation of Herculaneum and Pompeii. He is shown in this engraving with finds from Herculaneum.

started systematic work in 1748. Rich finds followed, but de Alcubierre was also far from a scientist. The good archaeologist is first and foremost a descriptive worker: he describes, classifies and analyses the objects he finds. But de Alcubierre, like the Prince d'Elboeuf, made no records when he removed objects from the site, and destroyed much in the process of excavation. Luckily, the Swiss architect, Karl Weber, was also present, and put in charge of the work at Herculaneum. He is one of the founding fathers of careful, scientific excavation; his uncovering of the luxurious Villa of the Papyri, in which a large collection of ancient writings was discovered in readable condition, was a model for future archaeologists' techniques. He classified and analysed his finds, dug systematically rather than in random tunnels, and constructed models and drawings of sites.

Giuseppe Fiorelli Further advances of this kind were made in the nineteenth century. The policy of digging tunnels at random, to find treasure, was abandoned, and emphasis was laid on a careful, detailed uncovering of Pompeii, block by block and house by house. A pioneer in this type of work was the superintendant of the excavation, Giuseppe Fiorelli, appointed in 1864. He made detailed maps, dividing Pompeii into nine *regiones* (town districts); within these, he marked individual *insulae* (blocks) and entrances. The House of the Vettii, for instance, is regio VI, insula 15, entrance 1.

A tavern sign, Pompeii. Underneath the sign is another which is an example of the location system developed by Giuseppe Fiorelli when he excavated the site. The sign is in regio (town district) VII, insula (block) IV.

Despite his careful work, Fiorelli became most famous for a useful, if rather macabre, technique for reconstituting the bodies of people killed during the eruption. The bodies had decomposed and left spaces in the ash. Fiorelli poured liquid plaster into the spaces, and this would harden, giving a perfect image of the body, even down to details of clothes, hair, and the facial expression at the moment of death. Some have claimed that it is an outrage against the dead to treat their bodies in this manner, but there is no doubt that much of our detailed knowledge of the last day of Pompeii is owed to Fiorelli's method.

Amedeo Maiuri

In the twentieth century, a large number of new techniques have come into use in archaeology. The traditional pick, shovel and trowel are now supplemented by compressed-air drills, electric saws, bulldozers, narrow-gauge railways and dump-trucks. The ground is minutely surveyed by aerial photography, and precise dates are established by radio-carbon analysis. All of these methods and more were

Fiorelli's excavations at Pompeii.

A model of the ruins of Pompeii in the National Archaeological Museum at Naples. In the foreground are the large theatre (left) and the covered theatre (right).

gradually introduced at Pompeii and Herculaneum, particularly during the long period from 1924 to 1961 when the distinguished archaeologist, Amedeo Maiuri, was superintendant of the excavations. Electric boring machines and mechanical shovels were among the first new methods introduced by him. Maiuri also displayed a determination to keep finds at Pompeii and Herculaneum, in the place where they were found, rather than remove them to the National Archaeological Museum at Naples, as had previously been common. In this way, he helped to preserve the integrity of the ancient sites, and enabled visitors to get an infinitely better impression of Roman life.

Today's problems   In spite of the great progress made under Maiuri and his successors, immense problems still remain, and the work at Pompeii and Herculaneum is far from complete. Only three-fifths of Pompeii has been uncovered, and much less of Herculaneum, where we do not yet have a clear view of the town plan, and have not yet uncovered the Forum which was the centre of every Roman town. The presence of the modern town of Ercolano above part of the site of Herculaneum, and the immensely hard nature of the solidified volcanic rock (*tufa*) that still covers much of the site, are among the reasons why less progress has been made here than at Pompeii.

Another problem is the upkeep of these fragile ancient sites. Despite Maiuri's care, by the end of his tenure, in 1961, Pompeii was falling into delapidation, and was overgrown with weeds. Much work in succeeding years was to go into preservation rather than further excavation: wood was treated, masonry propped up, wall-paintings were restored, and adequate security was provided against theft. Italy is a country with unparalleled remains from the period of its ancient greatness; yet its social problems (poverty, pollution, the underdeveloped south, for instance) mean there is a limited budget for preservation. Often the visitor receives the impression that there is neither the time nor the money to ensure that everything valuable from the ancient past is preserved. It is even possible for buildings which have been partly or wholly excavated to sink back beneath the earth, as has happened on several occasions. Above all, there is always a chance that Vesuvius will erupt again, burying the towns in a second oblivion.

Despite such problems, it is important to press on with the work, as it is certain that much of immense value still remains hidden in the earth. It is interesting to speculate on what may lie there. For instance, an ancient Roman novel, called the *Satyricon*, survives now only in fragments – but these have been published and are highly entertaining. The novel is thought to have been written by Petronius Arbiter, a courtier of the emperor Nero. He was forced by Nero to commit suicide in AD 66, but if he wrote his novel shortly before that date, there would have been just enough time before the destruction for the whole work to get into the library of a wealthy collector at Herculaneum or Pompeii. This would, of course, be a wonderful find, but even if it is not there, it is certain that other ancient objects of beauty and interest are still to be recovered.

What has the discovery of Pompeii and Herculaneum told us about ancient life?

The day on which Pompeii and Herculaneum were overwhelmed by catastrophe was a Day that Made History in a special sense. Although the disaster caused great interest at the centre of the Roman empire for a while, these had been only moderately important towns, rarely mentioned in historical records or ancient writing: no son of Pompeii had ever made himself a great name in Rome. The life of the empire went on for another four hundred years, affected only in the minutest way by the great tragedy. It was only after the rediscovery of the towns, many centuries later, that the full historical significance of 24th August, AD 79, became apparent.

By then, the towns had come to form a unique time capsule for humanity. Although ancient buildings and remains are to be found elsewhere, they are generally in a state of ruin, or so jumbled together with buildings from later eras that no

Bronze oil lamps. They are so similar that they probably come from the same workshop. The one on the left was found at Pompeii and the one on the right at Herculaneum.

picture can easily be formed of their original purpose or appearance. But Pompeii and Herculaneum are whole towns: two-storeyed buildings remain complete, with the pots and jugs still in the kitchen, and the meals, cooked so long ago, still waiting on the tables. It may still require an effort of the imagination to picture the towns as they were when Latin was the language of Italy, but only here is ancient life preserved in anything approaching completeness. They are truly, as the subtitle of one book calls them, "the living cities of the dead".

That two ancient towns have been preserved in this near-perfect state is especially valuable to us because of the nature of our other evidence about the ancient world. The historians and writers of ancient Greece and Rome did not have the interest in ordinary people and life that modern historians often have. They usually thought that it was only worth recording the lives of people who were distinguished in some way: by power, courage or wisdom. The result is that we only rarely get glimpses of what the great majority of people living in the Roman empire thought or felt, or how they lived. Evidence such as inscriptions on tombstones tells us something. In Egypt, because of the very dry climate, a large number of ancient letters and other documents on papyrus rolls have survived the centuries, and for this reason the people of ancient Egypt are better known to us than any other people from the Roman provinces. The only people of the ancient world known to us with comparable vividness are the ancient Italians, partly because of the unusually large amount of evidence that has survived about the city of Rome, but also because of Pompeii and Herculaneum.

Many of our general ideas about the lifestyle of the ancient world are based largely on the evidence available from the buried towns. This is true, for instance, in the matter of housing in towns. In Rome itself, ancient private houses do not survive, and their remains are found only in a few other places. But in Pompeii and Herculaneum, large numbers of private houses, together with the streets on which they stood, have been preserved almost intact. The main reason that the ancient Italian house is so much better known to us than the ancient Greek house (about which rather little is known) is the preservation of Pompeii and Herculaneum.

Homes It is largely from Pompeii and Herculaneum that we have gained our picture of the typical plan of the most common kind of house, the substantial *domus* or town-house, which was usually the property of reasonably wealthy people. Large

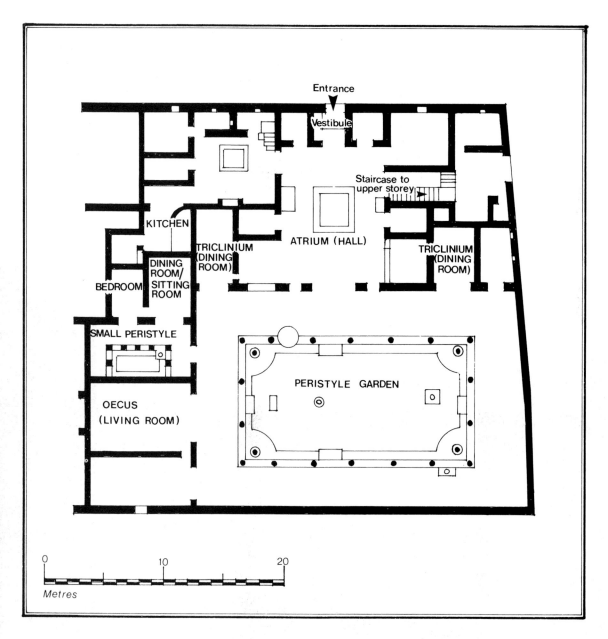

Entrance

Vestibule

Staircase to
upper storey

KITCHEN

TRICLINIUM
(DINING
ROOM)

ATRIUM (HALL)

TRICLINIUM
(DINING
ROOM)

DINING
ROOM/
SITTING
ROOM

BEDROOM

SMALL PERISTYLE

PERISTYLE GARDEN

OECUS
(LIVING ROOM)

0   10   20

Metres

and often splendidly decorated, a domus would often stay in the same family for centuries, becoming a symbol of family pride and continuity. These houses typically faced inwards, with very few windows looking out onto the street (see the plan of a Pompeian house): light was let into the main hall, or *atrium*, through an opening in the roof. Houses of this type

◁ *The House of the Vettii, one of the largest and most splendid houses in Pompeii, belonged to the Vettii brothers, Aulus Vettius Restitutus and Aulus Vettius Conviva, who, it has been suggested, may have been wealthy former slaves (freedmen). The plan of their house is typical of larger Pompeian mansions.*

The colonnaded courtyard, or peristyle, of the House of the Vettii, Pompeii.

were very often on two storeys. One important sign of the Greek influence in the area is the presence of large open colonnades (*peristyles*) at the back of the houses, embellished by gardens, statues and fountains: good places for eating supper outside in summer as a scented Mediterranean dusk came down.

Not all private homes were like this. Homes for the poor might well have been a room over a shop. In Rome, and elsewhere, people lived in large blocks of flats called *insulae* (islands), and some examples of these can be seen today at the ruins of the Roman port-town of Ostia. This type of accommodation does not seem to have spread to Pompeii by AD 79: some houses, however, were split into flats for different families, particularly during the last years of the town's life.

Paintings   Although the kitchens and bedrooms in even the larger houses were typically small, and lavatory arrangements often scarce, houses were generally much more beautiful than ours today, adorned with splendidly-coloured decoration, floor mosaics, and many wall-paintings, usually showing scenes from Greek mythology. In fact, a great deal of our detailed knowledge of ancient art is based on examples found at Pompeii and Herculaneum. Ancient Greek painting, for instance, except that done on vases, has hardly survived, although the Greeks themselves viewed it as one of their most

Frescoes in the House of the Vettii. Elaborate wall paintings were a feature of the town-houses of the wealthy.

Part of the painted frieze from the Hall of the Mysteries, Villa of the Mysteries, Pompeii. Although the content of the frieze is a matter of debate, the imagery relates to the cult of the Greek god Dionysus. The style of the painting relates very closely to ancient Greek painting.

important arts. But so many wall-paintings and examples of wall-decoration are available at Pompeii that art historians are able to distinguish four styles of painting, flourishing at different dates, which may have corresponded to periods in art history elsewhere. Some Pompeian paintings, in addition to their intrinsic artistic merit, give us valuable information about ancient life: the most famous paintings at Pompeii, those in the Villa of the Mysteries, showing initiation ceremonies into the worship of the Greek god Dionysus, are not only among the greatest works of art to have come down to us from the ancient world but also an important source of clues about a secretive cult.

Streets A fair amount of our knowledge of ancient street patterns comes from Pompeii and Herculaneum. We see that streets, in this part of the empire at least, had raised pavements on either side, and stepping stones were placed at intervals across the streets, so that people should not have to step in running water and rubbish. Streets were cobbled, and at Pompeii we can see many deep ruts made by traffic. The narrowness of ancient streets, and even major roads, always surprises us today. Those of Herculaneum seem, in general, hardly wide enough for a wagon or a chariot, while at Pompeii the streets, although slightly wider, are rarely more than four metres across. At most intersections, we can see public fountains with sculptured headstones, the stone worn away

A street in Pompeii. The stepping stones were for pedestrians to use in wet weather and were positioned so that the wheels of carts could pass on either side of them.

generations of people, ancient and modern, leaning over to drink.

Shops and hotels

Immensely interesting also are the remains of the various shops, workshops, hotels, restaurants and places of entertainment. Many of the best-preserved ancient buildings of all these types are at Pompeii. One hotel at Pompeii, for instance, has a large dining-room, a kitchen and six bedrooms. Some guests wrote their names in their bedrooms: two friends, Lucius and Primigenus, shared one room; four actors were in another. Pompeii also abounds in snack-bars (*thermopolia*): you can still see the food counters and the containers from which dishes were served. There was no large-scale industry in Pompeii, no factories, but there are plentiful remains of small businesses: dry-cleaning establishments, for instance, or many types of bakers.

A Pompeian thermopolium (snack-bar). Containers of food were placed in the holes in the counter.

Fortified towns   Pompeii has an impressive series of walls, towers and gates, which together make it the best surviving example of a fortified ancient Italian town. The earliest sections of wall still standing date from the fifth century BC, but in the second century they were strengthened, and in about 100 BC twelve towers were added. From these towers the defenders looked down when Pompeii was besieged by the Roman general Sulla, in 89 BC, during the revolt of much of Italy against Rome which is known as the Social War (*socii* is Latin for "allies"). Herculaneum, too, had walls, although less well-preserved: as life under the Roman empire became peaceful, grand houses were built on the promontory there, overlooking the sea, often using part of the walls for sun terraces. Outside the towns were large areas given over to cemeteries, because, by Roman custom, the dead could not be buried or cremated inside towns. At Pompeii, the Street of the Tombs, outside the Herculaneum Gate, is particularly well-preserved.

Interior of the amphitheatre, Pompeii.

Public buildings

Exterior of the amphitheatre, Pompeii. It was one of the first public buildings in Roman Italy to use the arcade as a decorative monumental feature.

The public buildings of Pompeii also have much to tell us, although here the position of the Italian towns is not so all-important, because numerous public buildings have survived in other parts of the empire too. The amphitheatre at Pompeii, however, is the earliest surviving from the empire (it was built around 80 BC), and it is a comparatively simple one: it lacks the vast network of underground rooms, to accommodate fighters and wild beasts, which is found at the Colosseum in Rome, built more than a century later.

The major public buildings, as in every Roman town, were in the large rectangular square called the Forum: temples, law-courts, council-offices, business headquarters. Among the earliest buildings in the Forum at Pompeii was the Temple of Apollo, originally built in the sixth century BC: a temple to a Greek god at that early date is a sign of the early influence of Greek colonists and settlers in this area of Italy.

The Temple of Apollo, one of the buildings in the Forum at Pompeii.

Real people It has been possible to identify some of the individuals represented in statues and paintings, and this has given us a closer knowledge of the men and women of ancient times. The bronze of the banker Lucius Caecilius Iucundus looks

It is possible that this portrait shows Paquius Proculus and his wife. The man holds a papyrus scroll, while his wife holds a stylus for writing on the two-leaved wooden tablet spread with wax which she holds in her left hand.

realistic, down to the large wart on his face. There is also a famous portrait of a young married couple, who had themselves painted holding a papyrus roll and wax tablet. It is possible that this painting may show the baker Paquius Proculus, who, despite his humble position, rose to become an *aedile* or town official of Pompeii. It was in the house of Paquius Proculus and his wife that seven children died in the upper room. This identification, however, has been disputed, particularly recently.

Graffiti Of all that has survived at Pompeii, it is the many casual graffiti and written notices which bring us closest to ancient Roman life: these tell us the very thoughts of Roman men, women and children. (There are many fewer graffiti in the more dignified town of Herculaneum.) Many of the graffiti relate to the annual elections for town officials, held every March and obviously followed by many Pompeians with passionate interest; of one candidate, it is approvingly remarked that *bonam panem fert* (he stands for good bread). Many other graffiti relate to private and personal life: it is touching to learn, for instance, that "Vibius Restitutus slept here alone and missed his dear Urbana". People write to their loved ones or admirers; one girl rejects a young man called Tertius on the simple grounds that he's too ugly. Obscene graffiti, both heterosexual and homosexual, are very common, as are injunctions not to foul the streets, or to beware of the dog (*cave canem*). Humour may not have changed much in 2000 years: one wit records, "Everyone writes on the walls except me", while a schoolboy humorist notes that if you don't like the works of Cicero you inevitably get whacked.

The town gladiators are the subject of much admiration: Celadus the Thracian is immortalized, for instance, as "the girls' heart-throb" (*suspirium puellarum*). Actors are almost equally popular: one group of people inform us that they are "companions of the Paris club" and another writes "Actius, our favourite, come back quickly". There are some signs of a high level of literary culture, in the many fragments of Roman poetry written on the walls (imagine modern graffitists quoting the works of T.S. Eliot!). Vergil, Tibullus, Lucretius and Ovid are among the poets represented; some of them, because of the height of the inscription, were obviously quoted by children anxious to show off what they had learnt at school. One adult quotes a charming fragment of folk poetry – or was it his own work?

> "Nothing lasts for ever,
> Though the sun shines gold,
> it must sink into the sea
> The moon has also disappeared
> which but now so brightly gleamed.
> So if the loved one rages,
> hold fast, this storm will soon yield,
> to the soft Zephyr."

Further reading

On Pompeii and Herculaneum

Marcel Brion, *Pompeii and Herculaneum: The Glory and the Grief*, Cardinal, 1973
E.C.C. Corti, *The destruction and resurrection of Pompeii and Herculaneum*, Routledge and Kegan Paul, 1951
J.J. Deiss, *Herculaneum: Italy's Buried Treasure*, Thames and Hudson, 1985
A. de Franciscis, *The Buried Cities: Pompeii and Herculaneum*, Orbis, 1978
Michael Grant, *Cities of Vesuvius*, Penguin, 1976
T. Kraus and L. von Matt, *Pompeii and Herculaneum: The Living Cities of the Dead*, Abrams, 1975
R. Seaford, *Pompeii*, Constable, 1978

On ancient Roman background

J.P.V.D. Balsdon, *Life and Leisure in Ancient Rome*, Bodley Head, 1969
Jérôme Carcopino, *Daily Life in Ancient Rome*, Peregrine, 1962
The Letters of the Younger Pliny, translation by Betty Radice, Penguin, 1963

On volcanoes and associated subjects

Darrell Weyman, *Tectonic Processes*, Allen and Unwin, 1981

DATE DUE

Brodart Co.   Cat. # 55 137 001